GO. MAKE. DISCIPLES.

GARRETT KAHRS

Copyright © 2021 by Garrett Kahrs

ISBN 13: 978-1-7357734-2-1

All rights reserved.

No part of this book may be reproduced in any form or by any electronic or mechanical means, including information storage and retrieval systems, without written permission from the author, except for the use of brief quotations in a book review.

CONTENTS

Introduction	vii
How to use this discipleship curriculum:	1
Week 1 Training: Salvation	4
DAY 1 BIBLE READING PLAN	7
DAY 2 BIBLE READING PLAN	9
DAY 3 BIBLE READING PLAN	11
DAY 4 BIBLE READING PLAN	13
DAY 5 BIBLE READING PLAN	15
DAY 6 BIBLE READING PLAN	17
DAY 7 BIBLE READING PLAN	19
Week 2 Training: Baptism	21
DAY 1 BIBLE READING PLAN	23
DAY 2 BIBLE READING PLAN	25
DAY 3 BIBLE READING PLAN	27
DAY 4 BIBLE READING PLAN	29
DAY 5 BIBLE READING PLAN	31
DAY 6 BIBLE READING PLAN	33
DAY 7 BIBLE READING PLAN	35
Week 3 Training: Bible Study	37
DAY 1 BIBLE READING PLAN	40
DAY 2 BIBLE READING PLAN	42
DAY 3 BIBLE READING PLAN	44
DAY 4 BIBLE READING PLAN	46
DAY 5 BIBLE READING PLAN	48
DAY 6 BIBLE READING PLAN	50
DAY 7 BIBLE READING PLAN	52
Week 4 Training: Prayer	54
DAY 1 BIBLE READING PLAN	57
DAY 2 BIBLE READING PLAN	59
DAY 3 BIBLE READING PLAN	61
DAY 4 BIBLE READING PLAN	63
DAY 5 BIBLE READING PLAN	65
DAY 6 BIBLE READING PLAN	67

DAY 7 BIBLE READING PLAN	69
Week 5 Training: Vision	71
DAY 1 BIBLE READING PLAN	75
DAY 2 BIBLE READING PLAN	77
DAY 3 BIBLE READING PLAN	79
DAY 4 BIBLE READING PLAN	81
DAY 5 BIBLE READING PLAN	83
DAY 6 BIBLE READING PLAN	85
DAY 7 BIBLE READING PLAN	87
Week 6 Training: Evangelism	89
DAY 1 BIBLE READING PLAN	93
DAY 2 BIBLE READING PLAN	95
DAY 3 BIBLE READING PLAN	97
DAY 4 BIBLE READING PLAN	99
DAY 5 BIBLE READING PLAN	101
DAY 6 BIBLE READING PLAN	103
DAY 7 BIBLE READING PLAN	105
Week 7 Training: Intimate Relationship	107
DAY 1 BIBLE READING PLAN	111
DAY 2 BIBLE READING PLAN	113
DAY 3 BIBLE READING PLAN	115
DAY 4 BIBLE READING PLAN	117
DAY 5 BIBLE READING PLAN	119
DAY 6 BIBLE READING PLAN	121
DAY 7 BIBLE READING PLAN	123
Week 8 Training: God the Father	125
DAY 1 BIBLE READING PLAN	129
DAY 2 BIBLE READING PLAN	131
DAY 3 BIBLE READING PLAN	133
DAY 4 BIBLE READING PLAN	135
DAY 5 BIBLE READING PLAN	137
DAY 6 BIBLE READING PLAN	139
DAY 7 BIBLE READING PLAN	141
Week 9 Training: Jesus	143
DAY 1 BIBLE READING PLAN	147
DAY 2 BIBLE READING PLAN	149
DAY 3 BIBLE READING PLAN	151
DAY 4 BIBLE READING PLAN	153
DAY 5 BIBLE READING PLAN	155
DAY 6 BIBLE READING PLAN	157
DAY 7 BIBLE READING PLAN	159

Week 10 Training: Holy Spirit	161
DAY 1 BIBLE READING PLAN	165
DAY 2 BIBLE READING PLAN	167
DAY 3 BIBLE READING PLAN	169
DAY 4 BIBLE READING PLAN	171
DAY 5 BIBLE READING PLAN	173
DAY 6 BIBLE READING PLAN	175
DAY 7 BIBLE READING PLAN	177
Week 11 Training: Community	179
DAY 1 BIBLE READING PLAN	183
DAY 2 BIBLE READING PLAN	185
DAY 3 BIBLE READING PLAN	187
DAY 4 BIBLE READING PLAN	189
DAY 5 BIBLE READING PLAN	191
DAY 6 BIBLE READING PLAN	193
DAY 7 BIBLE READING PLAN	195
Week 12 Training: Spiritual Disciplines	197
DAY 1 BIBLE READING PLAN	201
DAY 2 BIBLE READING PLAN	203
DAY 3 BIBLE READING PLAN	205
DAY 4 BIBLE READING PLAN	207
DAY 5 BIBLE READING PLAN	209
DAY 6 BIBLE READING PLAN	211
DAY 7 BIBLE READING PLAN	213
Week 13 Training: Grace	215
WHAT'S NEXT	217
Cheat Sheet: Week 1: Salvation	220
Cheat Sheet Week 2: Baptism	223
Cheat Sheet Week 3: Bible Study	225
Cheat Sheet Week 4: Prayer	226
Cheat Sheet Week 5: Vision	228
Cheat Sheet Week 6: Evangelism	231
Cheat Sheet Week 7: Intimate Relationship	233
Cheat Sheet Week 8: God the Father	235
Cheat Sheet Week 9: Jesus	237
Cheat Sheet Week 10: Holy Spirit	239
Cheat Sheet Week 11: Community	241
Cheat Sheet Week 12: Spiritual Disciplines	244
Cheat Sheet Week 13: Grace	247
Notes	249

INTRODUCTION

Many of us want to make disciples. We have been told at many events, church services, and conferences that in order to change the world we must go out and make disciples. But for some reason there is a divide between our desire to make disciples and seeing it actually happen in our lives.

This gap caused a deep sense of frustration as I started to run a young adult ministry in Kansas. I spent a year talking about making disciples from stage, over coffee, and at meal tables and saw not one person in our ministry making other disciples. I found that there was a separation between the amount of time I was talking about discipleship and how much time I was spending discipling others.

This dissatisfaction in my heart lead to the origin of this book. We started with a few of our students who wanted to be trained on how to make disciples. Soon we found out that we were onto something. God began to move in our hearts and we began to see fruit that we dreamed of!

Soon after starting one of our young adults told me, "This is the most fulfilled I have ever been in my walk with Christ." These words still echo in my ears as I wonder how many Christians are discontent in their faith because they don't know how to start making disciples. A few weeks later this same young adult sat down with one of her friends over a cup of coffee, shared the Gospel, and saw her friend respond to Jesus' invitation for a relationship. The best part? The story doesn't end there.

As her friend began her relationship with Christ she began to use this curriculum to show her how to read the bible, how to share her faith, and much more. Her friend was baptized shortly after and has continued to grow in her faith.

These are the stories I love to tell. God using regular, ordinary people for His glory all over the world. These stories happen all the time in all sorts of places. My hope and prayer is that this resource will help you write stories like this in your own life.

HOW TO USE THIS DISCIPLESHIP CURRICULUM:

Get the Leader Guide: Before you go any further. You can either buy the leader guide where you got this book or get my free leader guide at garrettkahrs.com/gmdleaderguide and it will help walk you through each of the weekly teachings. Without it this curriculum is without in depth teaching.

Daily Reading Plan: After you finish teaching the first lesson there is a daily reading plan for both you and the person you are going through this with to go through. Most people will not know how to read the Bible in this way so don't skip helping them learn how to go through the questions and steps outlined in each daily reading plan!

You may want to bring an extra Bible with you to your first meeting because they may not have one. If this is the case you will have to show them where each passage you are reading is. Take your time. Don't make them feel dumb for not knowing where Leviticus is because they have never opened the Word of God.

Or you can encourage them to download the Bible app on their phone. It will be much easier for them to find the passages they are looking to read on the app.

Life on Life: At the beginning of each weekly meeting open up with how each other are doing. Be honest, transparent how each other are doing. We will only grow together if we are doing life together.

You are also setting the example for them on how to live out our Christian faith. As you go they will go. Not only ask them questions about their life but be vulnerable about your struggles as well.

Accountability: This is a word that trips up many people including well-meaning Christians. We are meant to keep each other accountable. Accountability isn't calling people out on their mistakes but calling people up to the person God has called them to be. As you develop relationships with the people around you make sure not only are you helping them walk out the life God has intended for them. But they are also helping your life the life that God has designed for your life.

Ask questions about their intimacy with God. How their evangelistic outreach is going. Have they found someone to disciple yet? How is their prayer life and bible study going? Also share how you are doing in these areas.

Sharing the Gospel through your Testimony: In week 6 you will talk about evangelism. While there are many great ways to share the Gospel one of the most effective is sharing our testimony. You should begin by practicing sharing your own testimony in the group in 3 minutes. Then the next week as someone else to share their testimony.

If you are doing this training one on one, then just do this when they are ready to do it. There is no rush. You may need to help them write it if they have never done it before.

The hope of discipleship is not that we would just train more Christians to disciple Christians. The vision is that we would go out into the world and share the Gospel with nonbelievers and we would see new converts who have never followed Jesus before!

Casting Vision: This leader guide is to help you teach others to teach others. When you teach the person you are helping disciple, make sure they know they are to take this training and teach someone else. If we don't cast this vision, we will only make a first generation disciple that starts and stops with that person. For far too long we have poured into others without the expectation that they will teach others what they know. For many people, the next step they need to take in their spiritual maturity isn't learning more, it is to teach what they already know.

Celebrate the Wins: Celebrate every win, not just the "big" ones. Did someone start discipling someone else? Celebrate. Did one of your group members invite someone to church and get rejected? Celebrate! What we celebrate is what we will become. Let's celebrate obedience in discipleship not just when we think things are good.

I can remember the first time one of our group members was sharing the Gospel for the first time ever. She was the first person to share the Gospel out of our group. She messaged us all and we were praying for her. About an hour passed and she messaged us all as she led her friend to Christ. Not only did we celebrate in our group message we celebrated the next time we met in our discipleship group.

Ask Questions: I know that the are a ton of questions when it comes to discipleship and how to use this curriculum just for that reason I want you to be able to email me at garrett.kahrs@dealinghopeinc.com. Or message me on any social media app this is the quickest way to get ahold of me. You can find me on Facebook, Twitter, and Instagram @garrettkahrs.

I want to help you make disciples and am praying for a movement of discipleship to start where you are. I hope that this tool will be helpful for you to start fulfilling our calling to go make disciples!

WEEK 1 TRAINING: SALVATION

God's Design - Read Genesis 1

As God designed all of the world, He looked upon it and saw it was <u>Good</u>.

He designed us for a <u>relationship with him</u> and with a <u>mission in this world</u>.

Sin & Brokenness - Read Genesis 3

Because of Adam and Eve's <u>sin</u> we all face the <u>brokenness</u> and <u>consequences</u> of sin.

This is the reason for not only our own <u>personal sin</u>. But also, all of the <u>brokenness</u> that we see in the world today.

The result of sin is <u>Separation from God</u>.

Gospel - Read Luke 19:1-10

Jesus came to <u>Seek</u> and <u>Save</u> the <u>lost</u>.

Because of Jesus' <u>Sacrifice</u> on the <u>cross</u> we can now have an <u>intimate relationship</u> with God.

Read Romans 10:9-10

If we confess Jesus as our <u>Lord</u> and believe He was raised from the <u>dead</u> we will be saved.

Recover & Pursue - Read 2 Corinthians 5:16-21

If anyone is in Christ, they are a <u>new creation</u>. The <u>old</u> has gone, the <u>new</u> has come.

Because of our salvation our lives have been <u>changed</u>. This means we are able to no longer <u>live</u> the way we did before our lives with Christ!

This means we are free from our past and can discover the new life Christ offers us!

Grace - Read Ephesians 2:8-10

It is by __Grace__ that we have been saved.
We are created for __Good__ __Works__ which God prepared in advance for us to do.

Extra Studying: This week read the accounts of Jesus' death and resurrection.
   Matthew 27-28
   Mark 15-16
   Luke 23-24
   John 18-20

Questions:

Does God's love for you now seem greater because of Jesus' sacrifice for you? Why?

Have you placed your faith in Jesus' death and resurrection?

If not what is holding you back?

DAY 1 BIBLE READING PLAN

Read - Mark 1:1-20

Step 1: As you open your bible to Mark pray to open your time with God. Ask Him to show you truth as you read Scripture today.

Step 2: Watch this introduction to the book of Mark:
   http://bit.ly/markintro

Step 3: Read Mark 1:1-20 and underline any verses that stick out to you. Write down those verses here:

Step 4: Make observations:

Who is in this passage?

What is going on?

Where does it take place?

Step 5: Is there anything from this passage that is confusing? Write down any questions from this passage you have for your mentor, friend, or pastor?

Step 6: Application: What will you do differently in your life and walk with Christ because of this passage?

Step 7: Pray to close your time with God. Ask for Him to help you continue to understand scripture and to apply what you just read in His Word.

DAY 2 BIBLE READING PLAN

Read - Mark 1:21-39

Step 1: As you open your bible to Mark pray to open your time with God. Ask Him to show you truth as you read Scripture today.

Step 2: Read Mark 1:21-39 and underline any verses that stick out to you. Write down those verses here:

Step 3: Make observations:

Who is in this passage?

What is going on?

Where does it take place?

Step 4: Is there anything from this passage that is confusing? Write down any questions from this passage you have for your mentor, friend, or pastor?

Step 5: Application: What will you do differently in your life and walk with Christ because of this passage?

Step 6: Pray to close your time with God. Ask for Him to help you continue to understand scripture and to apply what you just read in His Word.

DAY 3 BIBLE READING PLAN

Read - Mark 1:40-2:12

Step 1: As you open your bible to Mark pray to open your time with God. Ask Him to show you truth as you read Scripture today.

Step 2: Read Mark 1:40-2:12 and underline any verses that stick out to you. Write down those verses here:

Step 3: Make observations:

Who is in this passage?

What is going on?

Where does it take place?

Step 4: Is there anything from this passage that is confusing? Write down any questions from this passage you have for your mentor, friend, or pastor?

Step 5: Application: What will you do differently in your life and walk with Christ because of this passage?

Step 6: Pray to close your time with God. Ask for Him to help you continue to understand scripture and to apply what you just read in His Word.

DAY 4 BIBLE READING PLAN

Read - Mark 2:13-28

Step 1: As you open your bible to Mark pray to open your time with God. Ask Him to show you truth as you read Scripture today.

Step 2: Read Mark 2:13-28 and underline any verses that stick out to you. Write down those verses here:

Step 3: Make observations:

Who is in this passage?

What is going on?

Where does it take place?

Step 4: Is there anything from this passage that is confusing? Write down any questions from this passage you have for your mentor, friend, or pastor?

Step 5: Application: What will you do differently in your life and walk with Christ because of this passage?

Step 6: Pray to close your time with God. Ask for Him to help you continue to understand scripture and to apply what you just read in His Word.

DAY 5 BIBLE READING PLAN

Read - Mark 3:1-19

Step 1: As you open your bible to Mark pray to open your time with God. Ask Him to show you truth as you read Scripture today.

Step 2: Read Mark 3:1-19 and underline any verses that stick out to you. Write down those verses here:

Step 3: Make observations:

Who is in this passage?

What is going on?

Where does it take place?

Step 4: Is there anything from this passage that is confusing? Write down any questions from this passage you have for your mentor, friend, or pastor?

Step 5: Application: What will you do differently in your life and walk with Christ because of this passage?

Step 6: Pray to close your time with God. Ask for Him to help you continue to understand scripture and to apply what you just read in His Word.

DAY 6 BIBLE READING PLAN

Read - Mark 3:20-35

Step 1: As you open your bible to Mark pray to open your time with God. Ask Him to show you truth as you read Scripture today.

Step 2: Read Mark 3:20-35 and underline any verses that stick out to you. Write down those verses here:

Step 3: Make observations:

Who is in this passage?

What is going on?

Where does it take place?

Step 4: Is there anything from this passage that is confusing? Write down any questions from this passage you have for your mentor, friend, or pastor?

Step 5: Application: What will you do differently in your life and walk with Christ because of this passage?

Step 6: Pray to close your time with God. Ask for Him to help you continue to understand scripture and to apply what you just read in His Word.

DAY 7 BIBLE READING PLAN

Read - Mark 4:1-20

Step 1: As you open your bible to Mark pray to open your time with God. Ask Him to show you truth as you read Scripture today.

Step 2: Read Mark 4:1-20 and underline any verses that stick out to you. Write down those verses here:

Step 3: Make observations:

Who is in this passage?

What is going on?

Where does it take place?

Step 4: Is there anything from this passage that is confusing? Write down any questions from this passage you have for your mentor, friend, or pastor?

Step 5: Application: What will you do differently in your life and walk with Christ because of this passage?

Step 6: Pray to close your time with God. Ask for Him to help you continue to understand scripture and to apply what you just read in His Word.

WEEK 2 TRAINING: BAPTISM

Read Matthew 3:13-17

Jesus _modeled_ the _importance_ of baptism for us.

Baptism is the _public_ declaration of our inward _commitment_

We are told in Matthew 28 that we supposed to _baptize_ all who are disciples of Jesus.

everyone who believes in Christ should be _baptized_.

Baptism is symbolic of our life with Christ

Us going into and under the water is symbolic of our
_____.

Us being raised out of the water is symbolic for our
_____.

Read Luke 23:32-43

After reading this passage do you believe you have to be baptized in order to be saved? Why or why not?

Question:

Have you been baptized? If not, are you ready to be baptized?

DAY 1 BIBLE READING PLAN

Read - Mark 4:21-34

Step 1: As you open your bible to Mark pray to open your time with God. Ask Him to show you truth as you read Scripture today.

Step 2: Read Mark 4:21-34 and underline any verses that stick out to you. Write down those verses here:

Step 3: Make observations:

Who is in this passage?

What is going on?

Where does it take place?

Step 4: Is there anything from this passage that is confusing? Write down any questions from this passage you have for your mentor, friend, or pastor?

Step 5: Application: What will you do differently in your life and walk with Christ because of this passage?

Step 6: Pray to close your time with God. Ask for Him to help you continue to understand scripture and to apply what you just read in His Word.

DAY 2 BIBLE READING PLAN

Read - Mark 4:35-5:20

Step 1: As you open your bible to Mark pray to open your time with God. Ask Him to show you truth as you read Scripture today.

Step 2: Read Mark 4:35-5:20 and underline any verses that stick out to you. Write down those verses here:

Step 3: Make observations:

Who is in this passage?

What is going on?

Where does it take place?

Step 4: Is there anything from this passage that is confusing? Write down any questions from this passage you have for your mentor, friend, or pastor?

Step 5: Application: What will you do differently in your life and walk with Christ because of this passage?

Step 6: Pray to close your time with God. Ask for Him to help you continue to understand scripture and to apply what you just read in His Word.

DAY 3 BIBLE READING PLAN

Read - Mark 5:21-34

Step 1: As you open your bible to Mark pray to open your time with God. Ask Him to show you truth as you read Scripture today.

Step 2: Read Mark 5:21-34 and underline any verses that stick out to you. Write down those verses here:

Step 3: Make observations:

Who is in this passage?

What is going on?

Where does it take place?

Step 4: Is there anything from this passage that is confusing? Write down any questions from this passage you have for your mentor, friend, or pastor?

Step 5: Application: What will you do differently in your life and walk with Christ because of this passage?

Step 6: Pray to close your time with God. Ask for Him to help you continue to understand scripture and to apply what you just read in His Word.

DAY 4 BIBLE READING PLAN

Read - Mark 5:35-6:6

Step 1: As you open your bible to Mark pray to open your time with God. Ask Him to show you truth as you read Scripture today.

Step 2: Read Mark 5:35-6:6 and underline any verses that stick out to you. Write down those verses here:

Step 3: Make observations:

Who is in this passage?

What is going on?

Where does it take place?

Step 4: Is there anything from this passage that is confusing? Write down any questions from this passage you have for your mentor, friend, or pastor?

Step 5: Application: What will you do differently in your life and walk with Christ because of this passage?

Step 6: Pray to close your time with God. Ask for Him to help you continue to understand scripture and to apply what you just read in His Word.

DAY 5 BIBLE READING PLAN

Read - Mark 6:7-29

Step 1: As you open your bible to Mark pray to open your time with God. Ask Him to show you truth as you read Scripture today.

Step 2: Read Mark 6:7-29 and underline any verses that stick out to you. Write down those verses here:

Step 3: Make observations:

Who is in this passage?

What is going on?

Where does it take place?

Step 4: Is there anything from this passage that is confusing? Write down any questions from this passage you have for your mentor, friend, or pastor?

Step 5: Application: What will you do differently in your life and walk with Christ because of this passage?

Step 6: Pray to close your time with God. Ask for Him to help you continue to understand scripture and to apply what you just read in His Word.

DAY 6 BIBLE READING PLAN

Read - Mark 6:30-44

Step 1: As you open your bible to Mark pray to open your time with God. Ask Him to show you truth as you read Scripture today.

Step 2: Read Mark 6:30-44 and underline any verses that stick out to you. Write down those verses here:

Step 3: Make observations:

Who is in this passage?

What is going on?

Where does it take place?

Step 4: Is there anything from this passage that is confusing? Write down any questions from this passage you have for your mentor, friend, or pastor?

Step 5: Application: What will you do differently in your life and walk with Christ because of this passage?

Step 6: Pray to close your time with God. Ask for Him to help you continue to understand scripture and to apply what you just read in His Word.

DAY 7 BIBLE READING PLAN

Read – Mark 6:45-56

Step 1: As you open your bible to Mark pray to open your time with God. Ask Him to show you truth as you read Scripture today.

Step 2: Read Mark 6:45-56 twice and underline any verses that stick out to you. Write down those verses here:

Step 3: Make observations:

Who is in this passage?

What is going on?

Where does it take place?

Step 4: Is there anything from this passage that is confusing? Write down any questions from this passage you have for your mentor, friend, or pastor?

Step 5: Application: What will you do differently in your life and walk with Christ because of this passage?

Step 6: Pray to close your time with God. Ask for Him to help you continue to understand scripture and to apply what you just read in His Word.

WEEK 3 TRAINING: BIBLE STUDY

Read 2 Timothy 3:16-17

Scripture is _____ for all we need to walk out our _____ in Jesus Christ.

Scripture is also our _____.

Read Psalms 119:147-148

_____ is essential for our relationship with _____.

Read Psalms 119:105

God's _____ will guide us in the _____ He _____ _____ to live.

TIPS FOR BIBLE READING:

Place: Choosing a place to do this is vital for consistency and you might need to change it up once in awhile

Time: Choosing a consistent time is essential for daily devotional time with God

Plan: Choose a book of the bible and read it at your own rate.

Questions:

Have you been able to take some daily time away to get into God's Word and spend time with Him?

If not, what is holding you back from spending time in God's Word?

Are there parts of scripture that cause a lot of confusion for you?

Here are a few Bible Study resources:

NIV Study Bible: http://bit.ly/nivvstudybible

Has life application and comments to help you understand the verses and passages that you read.

The Bible App: https://www.youversion.com/the-bible-app/

Has thousands of bibles reading plans that you can read on your phone

Constable Notes: http://planobiblechapel.org/constable-notes/

There are free commentaries for every book of the bible. The author goes into depth about the author and the setting of each book to help you understand the bible in greater depth.

DAY 1 BIBLE READING PLAN

Read - Mark 7:1-23

Step 1: As you open your bible to Mark pray to open your time with God. Ask Him to show you truth as you read Scripture today.

Step 2: Read Mark 7:1-23 and underline any verses that stick out to you. Write down those verses here:

Step 3: Make observations:

Who is in this passage?

What is going on?

Where does it take place?

Step 4: Is there anything from this passage that is confusing? Write down any questions from this passage you have for your mentor, friend, or pastor?

Step 5: Application: What will you do differently in your life and walk with Christ because of this passage?

Step 6: Pray to close your time with God. Ask for Him to help you continue to understand scripture and to apply what you just read in His Word.

DAY 2 BIBLE READING PLAN

Read - Mark 7:24-37

Step 1: As you open your bible to Mark pray to open your time with God. Ask Him to show you truth as you read Scripture today.

Step 2: Read Mark 7:24-37 and underline any verses that stick out to you. Write down those verses here:

Step 3: Make observations:

Who is in this passage?

What is going on?

Where does it take place?

Step 4: Is there anything from this passage that is confusing? Write down any questions from this passage you have for your mentor, friend, or pastor?

Step 5: Application: What will you do differently in your life and walk with Christ because of this passage?

Step 6: Pray to close your time with God. Ask for Him to help you continue to understand scripture and to apply what you just read in His Word.

DAY 3 BIBLE READING PLAN

Read - Mark 8:1-21

Step 1: As you open your bible to Mark pray to open your time with God. Ask Him to show you truth as you read Scripture today.

Step 2: Read Mark 8:1-21 and underline any verses that stick out to you. Write down those verses here:

Step 3: Make observations:

Who is in this passage?

What is going on?

Where does it take place?

Step 4: Is there anything from this passage that is confusing? Write down any questions from this passage you have for your mentor, friend, or pastor?

Step 5: Application: What will you do differently in your life and walk with Christ because of this passage?

Step 6: Pray to close your time with God. Ask for Him to help you continue to understand scripture and to apply what you just read in His Word.

DAY 4 BIBLE READING PLAN

Read - Mark 8:22-33

Step 1: As you open your bible to Mark pray to open your time with God. Ask Him to show you truth as you read Scripture today.

Step 2: Read Mark 8:22-33 and underline any verses that stick out to you. Write down those verses here:

Step 3: Make observations:

Who is in this passage?

What is going on?

Where does it take place?

Step 4: Is there anything from this passage that is confusing? Write down any questions from this passage you have for your mentor, friend, or pastor?

Step 5: Application: What will you do differently in your life and walk with Christ because of this passage?

Step 6: Pray to close your time with God. Ask for Him to help you continue to understand scripture and to apply what you just read in His Word.

DAY 5 BIBLE READING PLAN

Read - Mark 8:34-9:13

Step 1: As you open your bible to Mark pray to open your time with God. Ask Him to show you truth as you read Scripture today.

Step 2: Read Mark 8:34-9:13 and underline any verses that stick out to you. Write down those verses here:

Step 3: Make observations:

Who is in this passage?

What is going on?

Where does it take place?

Step 4: Is there anything from this passage that is confusing? Write down any questions from this passage you have for your mentor, friend, or pastor?

Step 5: Application: What will you do differently in your life and walk with Christ because of this passage?

Step 6: Pray to close your time with God. Ask for Him to help you continue to understand scripture and to apply what you just read in His Word.

DAY 6 BIBLE READING PLAN

Read - Mark 9:14-29

Step 1: As you open your bible to Mark pray to open your time with God. Ask Him to show you truth as you read Scripture today.

Step 2: Read Mark 9:14-29 and underline any verses that stick out to you. Write down those verses here:

Step 3: Make observations:

Who is in this passage?

What is going on?

Where does it take place?

Step 4: Is there anything from this passage that is confusing? Write down any questions from this passage you have for your mentor, friend, or pastor?

Step 5: Application: What will you do differently in your life and walk with Christ because of this passage?

Step 6: Pray to close your time with God. Ask for Him to help you continue to understand scripture and to apply what you just read in His Word.

DAY 7 BIBLE READING PLAN

Read - Mark 9:30-37

Step 1: As you open your bible to Mark pray to open your time with God. Ask Him to show you truth as you read Scripture today.

Step 2: Read Mark 9:30-37 and underline any verses that stick out to you. Write down those verses here:

Step 3: Make observations:

Who is in this passage?

What is going on?

Where does it take place?

Step 4: Is there anything from this passage that is confusing? Write down any questions from this passage you have for your mentor, friend, or pastor?

Step 5: Application: What will you do differently in your life and walk with Christ because of this passage?

Step 6: Pray to close your time with God. Ask for Him to help you continue to understand scripture and to apply what you just read in His Word.

WEEK 4 TRAINING: PRAYER

Read Luke 18:1

Jesus tells us we should _____ _____.

Read Matthew 6:5-15

Jesus _____ for us a _____ life of _____.

We _____ pray like _____ around us who are looking for _____.

_____ is designed to help us develop a deep _____ with God.

How then does Jesus tell us to pray?

Types of Prayers

_____ **Read Philippians 4:6-7**

_____ **Read 1 Timothy 2:1 & Philippians 4:6-7**

_____ **Read Psalm 135:3**

_____ **Read James 5:16** [1]

Questions:

How is your prayer life?

If you are unsatisfied in your prayer life, what can you change that will make it better?

Do you believe that prayer works? How has God answered your prayers?

Have you struggled treating prayer as a one way street? Where we only talk to God, but don't take the time to listen to Him?

Resources for developing a deeper prayer life:

Why Should we Pray?
   https://www.youtube.com/watch?v=9qUyesSg1R4

How to Spend an Hour in Prayer
   https://zume.training/how-to-spend-an-hour-in-prayer/

Book - Prayer: Experiencing Awe and Intimacy with God
   http://bit.ly/prayerkeller

Book - The Circle Maker
   https://www.markbatterson.com/books/the-circle-maker/

DAY 1 BIBLE READING PLAN

Read - Mark 9:38-50

Step 1: As you open your bible to Mark pray to open your time with God. Ask Him to show you truth as you read Scripture today.

Step 2: Read Mark 9:38-50 and underline any verses that stick out to you. Write down those verses here:

Step 3: Make observations:

Who is in this passage?

What is going on?

Where does it take place?

Step 4: Is there anything from this passage that is confusing? Write down any questions from this passage you have for your mentor, friend, or pastor?

Step 5: Application: What will you do differently in your life and walk with Christ because of this passage?

Step 6: Pray to close your time with God. Ask for Him to help you continue to understand scripture and to apply what you just read in His Word.

DAY 2 BIBLE READING PLAN

Read - Mark 10:1-16

Step 1: As you open your bible to Mark pray to open your time with God. Ask Him to show you truth as you read Scripture today.

Step 2: Read Mark 10:1-16 and underline any verses that stick out to you. Write down those verses here:

Step 3: Make observations:

Who is in this passage?

What is going on?

Where does it take place?

Step 4: Is there anything from this passage that is confusing? Write down any questions from this passage you have for your mentor, friend, or pastor?

Step 5: Application: What will you do differently in your life and walk with Christ because of this passage?

Step 6: Pray to close your time with God. Ask for Him to help you continue to understand scripture and to apply what you just read in His Word.

DAY 3 BIBLE READING PLAN

Read - Mark 10:17-31

Step 1: As you open your bible to Mark pray to open your time with God. Ask Him to show you truth as you read Scripture today.

Step 2: Read Mark 10:17-31 and underline any verses that stick out to you. Write down those verses here:

Step 3: Make observations:

Who is in this passage?

What is going on?

Where does it take place?

Step 4: Is there anything from this passage that is confusing? Write down any questions from this passage you have for your mentor, friend, or pastor?

Step 5: Application: What will you do differently in your life and walk with Christ because of this passage?

Step 6: Pray to close your time with God. Ask for Him to help you continue to understand scripture and to apply what you just read in His Word.

DAY 4 BIBLE READING PLAN

Read - Mark 10:32-45

Step 1: As you open your bible to Mark pray to open your time with God. Ask Him to show you truth as you read Scripture today.

Step 2: Read Mark 10:32-45 and underline any verses that stick out to you. Write down those verses here:

Step 3: Make observations:

Who is in this passage?

What is going on?

Where does it take place?

Step 4: Is there anything from this passage that is confusing? Write down any questions from this passage you have for your mentor, friend, or pastor?

Step 5: Application: What will you do differently in your life and walk with Christ because of this passage?

Step 6: Pray to close your time with God. Ask for Him to help you continue to understand scripture and to apply what you just read in His Word.

DAY 5 BIBLE READING PLAN

Read - Mark 11:1-25

Step 1: As you open your bible to Mark pray to open your time with God. Ask Him to show you truth as you read Scripture today.

Step 2: Read Mark 11:1-25 and underline any verses that stick out to you. Write down those verses here:

Step 3: Make observations:

Who is in this passage?

What is going on?

Where does it take place?

Step 4: Is there anything from this passage that is confusing? Write down any questions from this passage you have for your mentor, friend, or pastor?

Step 5: Application: What will you do differently in your life and walk with Christ because of this passage?

Step 6: Pray to close your time with God. Ask for Him to help you continue to understand scripture and to apply what you just read in His Word.

DAY 6 BIBLE READING PLAN

Read - Mark 11:27-12:12

Step 1: As you open your bible to Mark pray to open your time with God. Ask Him to show you truth as you read Scripture today.

Step 2: Read Mark 11:27-12:12 and underline any verses that stick out to you. Write down those verses here:

Step 3: Make observations:

Who is in this passage?

What is going on?

Where does it take place?

Step 4: Is there anything from this passage that is confusing? Write down any questions from this passage you have for your mentor, friend, or pastor?

Step 5: Application: What will you do differently in your life and walk with Christ because of this passage?

Step 6: Pray to close your time with God. Ask for Him to help you continue to understand scripture and to apply what you just read in His Word.

DAY 7 BIBLE READING PLAN

Read - Mark 12:13-34

Step 1: As you open your bible to Mark pray to open your time with God. Ask Him to show you truth as you read Scripture today.

Step 2: Read Mark 12:13-34 and underline any verses that stick out to you. Write down those verses here:

Step 3: Make observations:

Who is in this passage?

What is going on?

Where does it take place?

Step 4: Is there anything from this passage that is confusing? Write down any questions from this passage you have for your mentor, friend, or pastor?

Step 5: Application: What will you do differently in your life and walk with Christ because of this passage?

Step 6: Pray to close your time with God. Ask for Him to help you continue to understand scripture and to apply what you just read in His Word.

WEEK 5 TRAINING: VISION

Read Matthew 4:18-22

One of the __*first*__ things that Jesus did after his baptism (Matthew 3) was go find __*disciples*__.

Jesus told them __*follow me*__ and I will make you __*fishers*__ of __*men*__.

Jesus is describing to them the two biggest things when it comes to discipleship:

1) __*follow me*__

2) _____ _____

Read Matthew 28:18-20

At the end of Jesus' life on earth we see him once again showing the disciples the importance of discipleship.

Because all __Authority__ has been given to Jesus we are supposed to __make__ / __disciples__.

What does making disciples look like according to this passage?
1) __make disciples__
2) __baptize them__
3) __teach them to obey His commands__

Jesus leaves us with a promise at the end of this passage what is it?

Read Acts 1:1-11

Where was God sending the disciples?
__Jerusalem__ - Hometown Maxwell
__Judea__ - State of Province
__Samaria__ - Neighboring States/Provinces
__The ends of the earth__ - The entire world

Read 2 Timothy 2:1-2

Vision for discipleship is to the __4th__ generation

- __Paul__ Discipled Timothy
- Timothy disciples __reliable people__
- Reliable people disciple __others__

What if 10 people started discipled 2 people a year?

How many people would we reach in?
  5 years: __320 - Half of Hays Kansas__
  10 years: __10,240 - Half of Hays Kansas__
  25 years: __335 Millions ~ Pop of USA__
  30 years: __Over 7 billion - Pop of World__

Questions:

Do you believe that you can make disciples? Why or why not?
__Yes and no, I'm not good enough.__

How does seeing God's vision of discipleship make you feel? Does God's vision make you believe you are called to be a part of something bigger than yourself?

Are you ready to say yes to Christ's invitation to make disciples? If not why is that?

Prayer Time:

Ask God to share with you a few people who might be willing to be discipled. Write their names below:

1)

2)

3)

DAY 1 BIBLE READING PLAN

Read - Mark 12:35-44

Step 1: As you open your bible to Mark pray to open your time with God. Ask Him to show you truth as you read Scripture today.

Step 2: Read Mark 12:35-44 and underline any verses that stick out to you. Write down those verses here:

Step 3: Make observations:

Who is in this passage?

What is going on?

Where does it take place?

Step 4: Is there anything from this passage that is confusing? Write down any questions from this passage you have for your mentor, friend, or pastor?

Step 5: Application: What will you do differently in your life and walk with Christ because of this passage?

Step 6: Pray to close your time with God. Ask for Him to help you continue to understand scripture and to apply what you just read in His Word.

DAY 2 BIBLE READING PLAN

Read - Mark 13:1-20

Step 1: As you open your bible to Mark pray to open your time with God. Ask Him to show you truth as you read Scripture today.

Step 2: Read Mark 13:1-20 and underline any verses that stick out to you. Write down those verses here:

Step 3: Make observations:

Who is in this passage?

What is going on?

Where does it take place?

Step 4: Is there anything from this passage that is confusing? Write down any questions from this passage you have for your mentor, friend, or pastor?

Step 5: Application: What will you do differently in your life and walk with Christ because of this passage?

Step 6: Pray to close your time with God. Ask for Him to help you continue to understand scripture and to apply what you just read in His Word. "

DAY 3 BIBLE READING PLAN

Read - Mark 13:21-37

Step 1: As you open your bible to Mark pray to open your time with God. Ask Him to show you truth as you read Scripture today.

Step 2: Read Mark 13:21-37 and underline any verses that stick out to you. Write down those verses here:

Step 3: Make observations:

Who is in this passage?

What is going on?

Where does it take place?

Step 4: Is there anything from this passage that is confusing? Write down any questions from this passage you have for your mentor, friend, or pastor?

Step 5: Application: What will you do differently in your life and walk with Christ because of this passage?

Step 6: Pray to close your time with God. Ask for Him to help you continue to understand scripture and to apply what you just read in His Word.

DAY 4 BIBLE READING PLAN

Read - Mark 14:1-26

Step 1: As you open your bible to Mark pray to open your time with God. Ask Him to show you truth as you read Scripture today.

Step 2: Read Mark 14:1-26 and underline any verses that stick out to you. Write down those verses here:

Step 3: Make observations:

Who is in this passage?

What is going on?

Where does it take place?

Step 4: Is there anything from this passage that is confusing? Write down any questions from this passage you have for your mentor, friend, or pastor?

Step 5: Application: What will you do differently in your life and walk with Christ because of this passage?

Step 6: Pray to close your time with God. Ask for Him to help you continue to understand scripture and to apply what you just read in His Word.

DAY 5 BIBLE READING PLAN

Read - Mark 14:27-42

Step 1: As you open your bible to Mark pray to open your time with God. Ask Him to show you truth as you read Scripture today.

Step 2: Read Mark 14:27-42 and underline any verses that stick out to you. Write down those verses here:

Step 3: Make observations:

Who is in this passage?

What is going on?

Where does it take place?

Step 4: Is there anything from this passage that is confusing? Write down any questions from this passage you have for your mentor, friend, or pastor?

Step 5: Application: What will you do differently in your life and walk with Christ because of this passage?

Step 6: Pray to close your time with God. Ask for Him to help you continue to understand scripture and to apply what you just read in His Word.

DAY 6 BIBLE READING PLAN

Read - Mark 14:43-65

Step 1: As you open your bible to Mark pray to open your time with God. Ask Him to show you truth as you read Scripture today.

Step 2: Read Mark 14:43-65 and underline any verses that stick out to you. Write down those verses here:

Step 3: Make observations:

Who is in this passage?

What is going on?

Where does it take place?

Step 4: Is there anything from this passage that is confusing? Write down any questions from this passage you have for your mentor, friend, or pastor?

Step 5: Application: What will you do differently in your life and walk with Christ because of this passage?

Step 6: Pray to close your time with God. Ask for Him to help you continue to understand scripture and to apply what you just read in His Word.

DAY 7 BIBLE READING PLAN

Read - Mark 14:66-15:15

Step 1: As you open your bible to Mark pray to open your time with God. Ask Him to show you truth as you read Scripture today.

Step 2: Read Mark 14:66-15:15 and underline any verses that stick out to you. Write down those verses here:

Step 3: Make observations:

Who is in this passage?

What is going on?

Where does it take place?

Step 4: Is there anything from this passage that is confusing? Write down any questions from this passage you have for your mentor, friend, or pastor?

Step 5: Application: What will you do differently in your life and walk with Christ because of this passage?

Step 6: Pray to close your time with God. Ask for Him to help you continue to understand scripture and to apply what you just read in His Word.

WEEK 6 TRAINING: EVANGELISM

Read Matthew 13:1-23

What are the 4 types of Seeds?

1)

2)

3)

4)

_____ looks a lot like us sowing seeds in the _____ around us.

Don't be _____ as you share the Gospel if this _____ comes to life.

As you share the Gospel people will be hard hearted towards it. Some will accept it readily and then will fall away later. And some will grow deep roots and grow the way you want them too!

Our job is not to worry about _____ _____ but to _____ _____.

Read John 4:1-42

No one can argue with your _____.

What if sharing the Gospel is as easy as sharing your _____.

Read Luke 10:1-20

Sharing the _____ simply starts with a _____ with Jesus.

Here is how to share the Gospel in your testimony:

1) Talk about what your life was like before Christ.

2) Describe how you came to hear the Gospel. Tell them how God opened your heart to the truth of Jesus dying on the cross for our sins and being raised to life 3 days later?

3) Finally, share about how your life has changed since your conversion. What is different about your life?

Who are the people God is calling you to reach with the hope of the Gospel? Write them in the space below:

1)

2)

3)

Don't be surprised if God brings someone into your life that isn't on this list!

Some other great resources on how to share the Gospel:

Three Circles:
  https://bit.ly/three3circles

Gospel Appointments:
  https://gospelappointments.com

How to Talk to With People who Don't Know Jesus
   http://bit.ly/howtotalkwnonbelievers

Book - *Master Plan of Evangelism*
   http://bit.ly/mstplnevangelism

DAY 1 BIBLE READING PLAN

Read - Mark 15:16-39

Step 1: As you open your bible to Mark pray to open your time with God. Ask Him to show you truth as you read Scripture today.

Step 2: Read Mark 15:16-39 and underline any verses that stick out to you. Write down those verses here:

Step 3: Make observations:

Who is in this passage?

What is going on?

Where does it take place?

Step 4: Is there anything from this passage that is confusing? Write down any questions from this
    passage you have for your mentor, friend, or pastor?

Step 5: Application: What will you do differently in your life and walk with Christ because of this passage?

Step 6: Pray to close your time with God. Ask for Him to help you continue to understand scripture and to apply what you just read in His Word.

DAY 2 BIBLE READING PLAN

Read - Mark 15:40-47

Step 1: As you open your bible to Mark pray to open your time with God. Ask Him to show you truth as you read Scripture today.

Step 2: Read Mark 15:40-47 and underline any verses that stick out to you. Write down those verses here:

Step 3: Make observations:

Who is in this passage?

What is going on?

Where does it take place?

Step 4: Is there anything from this passage that is confusing? Write down any questions from this passage you have for your mentor, friend, or pastor?

Step 5: Application: What will you do differently in your life and walk with Christ because of this passage?

Step 6: Pray to close your time with God. Ask for Him to help you continue to understand scripture and to apply what you just read in His Word.

DAY 3 BIBLE READING PLAN

Read - Mark 16:1-8

Step 1: As you open your bible to Mark pray to open your time with God. Ask Him to show you truth as you read Scripture today.

Step 2: Read Mark 16:1-8 and underline any verses that stick out to you. Write down those verses here:

Step 3: Make observations:

Who is in this passage?

What is going on?

Where does it take place?

Step 4: Is there anything from this passage that is confusing? Write down any questions from this passage you have for your mentor, friend, or pastor?

Step 5: Application: What will you do differently in your life and walk with Christ because of this passage?

Step 6: Pray to close your time with God. Ask for Him to help you continue to understand scripture and to apply what you just read in His Word.

DAY 4 BIBLE READING PLAN

Read - Mark 16:9-14

Step 1: As you open your bible to Mark pray to open your time with God. Ask Him to show you truth as you read Scripture today.

Step 2: Read Mark 16:9-14 and underline any verses that stick out to you. Write down those verses here:

Step 3: Make observations:

Who is in this passage?

What is going on?

Where does it take place?

Step 4: Is there anything from this passage that is confusing? Write down any questions from this passage you have for your mentor, friend, or pastor?

Step 5: Application: What will you do differently in your life and walk with Christ because of this passage?

Step 6: Pray to close your time with God. Ask for Him to help you continue to understand scripture and to apply what you just read in His Word.

DAY 5 BIBLE READING PLAN

Read - Mark 16:15-20

Step 1: As you open your bible to Mark pray to open your time with God. Ask Him to show you truth as you read Scripture today.

Step 2: Read Mark 16:15-20 and underline any verses that stick out to you. Write down those verses here:

Step 3: Make observations:

Who is in this passage?

What is going on?

Where does it take place?

Step 4: Is there anything from this passage that is confusing? Write down any questions from this passage you have for your mentor, friend, or pastor?

Step 5: Application: What will you do differently in your life and walk with Christ because of this passage?

Step 6: Pray to close your time with God. Ask for Him to help you continue to understand scripture and to apply what you just read in His Word.

DAY 6 BIBLE READING PLAN

Read - Ephesians 1:1-6

Step 1: As you open your bible to Mark pray to open your time with God. Ask Him to show you truth as you read Scripture today.

Step 2: Watch this introduction video to Ephesians: https://bit.ly/ephesiansintro

Step 3: Read Ephesians 1:1-6 and underline any verses that stick out to you. Write down those verses here:

Step 4: Make observations:

Who is in this passage?

What is going on?

Where does it take place?

Step 5: Is there anything from this passage that is confusing? Write down any questions from this passage you have for your mentor, friend, or pastor?

Step 6: Application: What will you do differently in your life and walk with Christ because of this passage?

Step 7: Pray to close your time with God. Ask for Him to help you continue to understand scripture and to apply what you just read in His Word.

DAY 7 BIBLE READING PLAN

Read – Ephesians 1:7-10

Step 1: As you open your bible to Mark pray to open your time with God. Ask Him to show you truth as you read Scripture today.

Step 2: Read Ephesians 1:7-10 and underline any verses that stick out to you. Write down those verses here:

Step 3: Make observations:

Who is in this passage?

What is going on?

Where does it take place?

Step 4: Is there anything from this passage that is confusing? Write down any questions from this passage you have for your mentor, friend, or pastor?

Step 5: Application: What will you do differently in your life and walk with Christ because of this passage?

Step 6: Pray to close your time with God. Ask for Him to help you continue to understand scripture and to apply what you just read in His Word.

WEEK 7 TRAINING: INTIMATE RELATIONSHIP

Read John 5:16-23

Jesus _____ for us what an _____ _____ with God can look like.

Jesus again connects our _____ with God with our _____.

This doesn't mean that our _____ will _____ _____. But it does mean that because of our _____ for God we will walk in _____.

Read John 15:1-17

What does Jesus use to illustrate our relationship with Him?

What do you think it means to abide (remain)?

_____ is an _____ _____, _____ relationship with God.

Once again Jesus connects our _____ to Him to our _____ with Him.

Questions:

Does this change any way you have viewed obedience to God in the past?

Is there anything in our life that isn't bearing fruit that we need to cut off? What is it and how can you remove it from your life?

Want to go deeper in your walk with Christ? Here are some more resources:

Book - *Practicing the Presence of God*
http://bit.ly/practicingthepresence

Book - *Crazy Love*
   http://bit.ly/crzylovefc

Book - *#Relationshipgoals: Discovering God's Desire and Design for Relationship With Him*
   http://bit.ly/relationshipwgod

DAY 1 BIBLE READING PLAN

Read - Ephesians 1:11-14

Step 1: As you open your bible to Mark pray to open your time with God. Ask Him to show you truth as you read Scripture today.

Step 2: Read Ephesians 1:11-14 and underline any verses that stick out to you. Write down those verses here:

Step 3: Make observations:

Who is in this passage?

What is going on?

Where does it take place?

Step 4: Is there anything from this passage that is confusing? Write down any questions from this passage you have for your mentor, friend, or pastor?

Step 5: Application: What will you do differently in your life and walk with Christ because of this passage?

Step 6: Pray to close your time with God. Ask for Him to help you continue to understand scripture and to apply what you just read in His Word.

DAY 2 BIBLE READING PLAN

Read - Ephesians 1:15-23

Step 1: As you open your bible to Mark pray to open your time with God. Ask Him to show you truth as you read Scripture today.

Step 2: Read Ephesians 1:15-23 and underline any verses that stick out to you. Write down those verses here:

Step 3: Make observations:

Who is in this passage?

What is going on?

Where does it take place?

Step 4: Is there anything from this passage that is confusing? Write down any questions from this passage you have for your mentor, friend, or pastor?

Step 5: Application: What will you do differently in your life and walk with Christ because of this passage?

Step 6: Pray to close your time with God. Ask for Him to help you continue to understand scripture and to apply what you just read in His Word.

DAY 3 BIBLE READING PLAN

Read - Ephesians 2:1-7

Step 1: As you open your bible to Mark pray to open your time with God. Ask Him to show you truth as you read Scripture today.

Step 2: Read Ephesians 2:1-7 and underline any verses that stick out to you. Write down those verses here:

Step 3: Make observations:

Who is in this passage?

What is going on?

Where does it take place?

Step 4: Is there anything from this passage that is confusing? Write down any questions from this passage you have for your mentor, friend, or pastor?

Step 5: Application: What will you do differently in your life and walk with Christ because of this passage?

Step 6: Pray to close your time with God. Ask for Him to help you continue to understand scripture and to apply what you just read in His Word.

DAY 4 BIBLE READING PLAN

Read - Ephesians 2:8-10

Step 1: As you open your bible to Mark pray to open your time with God. Ask Him to show you truth as you read Scripture today.

Step 2: Read Ephesians 2:8-10 and underline any verses that stick out to you. Write down those verses here:

Step 3: Make observations:

Who is in this passage?

What is going on?

Where does it take place?

Step 4: Is there anything from this passage that is confusing? Write down any questions from this passage you have for your mentor, friend, or pastor?

Step 5: Application: What will you do differently in your life and walk with Christ because of this passage?

Step 6: Pray to close your time with God. Ask for Him to help you continue to understand scripture and to apply what you just read in His Word.

DAY 5 BIBLE READING PLAN

Read - Ephesians 2:11-13

Step 1: As you open your bible to Mark pray to open your time with God. Ask Him to show you truth as you read Scripture today.

Step 2: Read Ephesians 2:11-13 and underline any verses that stick out to you. Write down those verses here:

Step 3: Make observations:

Who is in this passage?

What is going on?

Where does it take place?

Step 4: Is there anything from this passage that is confusing? Write down any questions from this passage you have for your mentor, friend, or pastor?

Step 5: Application: What will you do differently in your life and walk with Christ because of this passage?

Step 6: Pray to close your time with God. Ask for Him to help you continue to understand scripture and to apply what you just read in His Word.

DAY 6 BIBLE READING PLAN

Read - Ephesians 2:14-18

Step 1: As you open your bible to Mark pray to open your time with God. Ask Him to show you truth as you read Scripture today.

Step 2: Read Ephesians 2:14-18 and underline any verses that stick out to you. Write down those verses here:

Step 3: Make observations:

Who is in this passage?

What is going on?

Where does it take place?

Step 4: Is there anything from this passage that is confusing? Write down any questions from this passage you have for your mentor, friend, or pastor?

Step 5: Application: What will you do differently in your life and walk with Christ because of this passage?

Step 6: Pray to close your time with God. Ask for Him to help you continue to understand scripture and to apply what you just read in His Word.

DAY 7 BIBLE READING PLAN

Read - Ephesians 2:19-22

Step 1: As you open your bible to Mark pray to open your time with God. Ask Him to show you truth as you read Scripture today.

Step 2: Read Ephesians 2:19-22 and underline any verses that stick out to you. Write down those verses here:

Step 3: Make observations:

Who is in this passage?

What is going on?

Where does it take place?

Step 4: Is there anything from this passage that is confusing? Write down any questions from this passage you have for your mentor, friend, or pastor?

Step 5: Application: What will you do differently in your life and walk with Christ because of this passage?

Step 6: Pray to close your time with God. Ask for Him to help you continue to understand scripture and to apply what you just read in His Word.

WEEK 8 TRAINING: GOD THE FATHER

What was your father like? Did you have one? Was he a good dad?

How has your earthly father impacted your view of God the Father?

Read 1 John 3:1

We have a Heavenly Father who _____ His _____ on us.

Read Matthew 7:7-12

What stands out to you about God the Father in this passage? Does this change your perspective of Him?

Read Luke 15:11-24

No matter _____ _____ you have fallen away from God the Father, He will always _____ _____ _____.

Read Proverbs 3:11-12

In His _____ God will _____ His Children.

Questions:

How does the training you went through today change the way you view God the Father?

How have you viewed God's discipline in the past?

How does God's loving discipline change the way you view His discipline as a whole?

Here are a few resources to go deeper:

Book - *Delighting in the Trinity*
http://bit.ly/delightintrinity

Book - *God Distorted*
   http://bit.ly/Goddistorted

Book - *Knowing God*
   http://bit.ly/knowgodbook

DAY 1 BIBLE READING PLAN

Read - Ephesians 3:1-6

Step 1: As you open your bible to Mark pray to open your time with God. Ask Him to show you truth as you read Scripture today.

Step 2: Read Ephesians 3:1-6 and underline any verses that stick out to you. Write down those verses here:

Step 3: Make observations:

Who is in this passage?

What is going on?

Where does it take place?

Step 4: Is there anything from this passage that is confusing? Write down any questions from this passage you have for your mentor, friend, or pastor?

Step 5: Application: What will you do differently in your life and walk with Christ because of this passage?

Step 6: Pray to close your time with God. Ask for Him to help you continue to understand scripture and to apply what you just read in His Word.

DAY 2 BIBLE READING PLAN

Read - Ephesians 3:7-13

Step 1: As you open your bible to Mark pray to open your time with God. Ask Him to show you truth as you read Scripture today.

Step 2: Read Ephesians 3:7-13 and underline any verses that stick out to you. Write down those verses here:

Step 3: Make observations:

Who is in this passage?

What is going on?

Where does it take place?

Step 4: Is there anything from this passage that is confusing? Write down any questions from this passage you have for your mentor, friend, or pastor?

Step 5: Application: What will you do differently in your life and walk with Christ because of this passage?

Step 6: Pray to close your time with God. Ask for Him to help you continue to understand scripture and to apply what you just read in His Word.

DAY 3 BIBLE READING PLAN

Read - Ephesians 3:14-21

Step 1: As you open your bible to Mark pray to open your time with God. Ask Him to show you truth as you read Scripture today.

Step 2: Read Ephesians 3:14-21 and underline any verses that stick out to you. Write down those verses here:

Step 3: Make observations:

Who is in this passage?

What is going on?

Where does it take place?

Step 4: Is there anything from this passage that is confusing? Write down any questions from this passage you have for your mentor, friend, or pastor?

Step 5: Application: What will you do differently in your life and walk with Christ because of this passage?

Step 6: Pray to close your time with God. Ask for Him to help you continue to understand scripture and to apply what you just read in His Word.

DAY 4 BIBLE READING PLAN

Read - Ephesians 4:1-6

Step 1: As you open your bible to Mark pray to open your time with God. Ask Him to show you truth as you read Scripture today.

Step 2: Read Ephesians 4:1-6 and underline any verses that stick out to you. Write down those verses here:

Step 3: Make observations:

Who is in this passage?

What is going on?

Where does it take place?

Step 4: Is there anything from this passage that is confusing? Write down any questions from this passage you have for your mentor, friend, or pastor?

Step 5: Application: What will you do differently in your life and walk with Christ because of this passage?

Step 6: Pray to close your time with God. Ask for Him to help you continue to understand scripture and to apply what you just read in His Word.

DAY 5 BIBLE READING PLAN

Read - Ephesians 4:7-13

Step 1: As you open your bible to Mark pray to open your time with God. Ask Him to show you truth as you read Scripture today.

Step 2: Read Ephesians 4:7-13 and underline any verses that stick out to you. Write down those verses here:

Step 3: Make observations:

Who is in this passage?

What is going on?

Where does it take place?

Step 4: Is there anything from this passage that is confusing? Write down any questions from this passage you have for your mentor, friend, or pastor?

Step 5: Application: What will you do differently in your life and walk with Christ because of this passage?

Step 6: Pray to close your time with God. Ask for Him to help you continue to understand scripture and to apply what you just read in His Word.

DAY 6 BIBLE READING PLAN

Read - Ephesians 4:14-16

Step 1: As you open your bible to Mark pray to open your time with God. Ask Him to show you truth as you read Scripture today.

Step 2: Read Ephesians 4:14-16 and underline any verses that stick out to you. Write down those verses here:

Step 3: Make observations:

Who is in this passage?

What is going on?

Where does it take place?

Step 4: Is there anything from this passage that is confusing? Write down any questions from this passage you have for your mentor, friend, or pastor?

Step 5: Application: What will you do differently in your life and walk with Christ because of this passage?

Step 6: Pray to close your time with God. Ask for Him to help you continue to understand scripture and to apply what you just read in His Word.

DAY 7 BIBLE READING PLAN

Read – Ephesians 4:17-24

Step 1: As you open your bible to Mark pray to open your time with God. Ask Him to show you truth as you read Scripture today.

Step 2: Read Ephesians 4:17-24 and underline any verses that stick out to you. Write down those verses here:

Step 3: Make observations:

Who is in this passage?

What is going on?

Where does it take place?

Step 4: Is there anything from this passage that is confusing? Write down any questions from this passage you have for your mentor, friend, or pastor?

Step 5: Application: What will you do differently in your life and walk with Christ because of this passage?

Step 6: Pray to close your time with God. Ask for Him to help you continue to understand scripture and to apply what you just read in His Word.

WEEK 9 TRAINING: JESUS

Read Matthew 16:13-21

There is a _____ between the way the _____ views Jesus and who He really is.

Read John 1:35-39

Jesus is our _____.

Read Philippians 2:8-11, Revelation 19:16

Jesus is our _____ _____ _____.

Read John 3:16, 1 John 4:14

Jesus is our _____.

Read John 10:1-18

Jesus is our _____.

Read John 1:1, 1:14, Romans 9:5

Jesus is _____.

Questions:

What stands out to you about Jesus from today's training?

How have you viewed Jesus much more like the world than how we are supposed to view Him?

Here are a few resources to go deeper:

Book - Simply Jesus
   http://bit.ly/simplyjesusbook

Book - Sitting at the Feet of Rabbi Jesus
   http://bit.ly/rabbibookjesus

Book - Four Portraits One Jesus
https://bit.ly/onejesus

DAY 1 BIBLE READING PLAN

Read - Ephesians 4:25-28

Step 1: As you open your bible to Mark pray to open your time with God. Ask Him to show you truth as you read Scripture today.

Step 2: Read Ephesians 4:25-28 and underline any verses that stick out to you. Write down those verses here:

Step 3: Make observations:

Who is in this passage?

What is going on?

Where does it take place?

Step 4: Is there anything from this passage that is confusing? Write down any questions from this passage you have for your mentor, friend, or pastor?

Step 5: Application: What will you do differently in your life and walk with Christ because of this passage?

Step 6: Pray to close your time with God. Ask for Him to help you continue to understand scripture and to apply what you just read in His Word.

DAY 2 BIBLE READING PLAN

Read - Ephesians 4:29-32

Step 1: As you open your bible to Mark pray to open your time with God. Ask Him to show you truth as you read Scripture today.

Step 2: Read Ephesians 4:29-32 and underline any verses that stick out to you. Write down those verses here:

Step 3: Make observations:

Who is in this passage?

What is going on?

Where does it take place?

Step 4: Is there anything from this passage that is confusing? Write down any questions from this passage you have for your mentor, friend, or pastor?

Step 5: Application: What will you do differently in your life and walk with Christ because of this passage?

Step 6: Pray to close your time with God. Ask for Him to help you continue to understand scripture and to apply what you just read in His Word.

DAY 3 BIBLE READING PLAN

Read - Ephesians 5:1-7

Step 1: As you open your bible to Mark pray to open your time with God. Ask Him to show you truth as you read Scripture today.

Step 2: Read Ephesians 5:1-7 and underline any verses that stick out to you. Write down those verses here:

Step 3: Make observations:

Who is in this passage?

What is going on?

Where does it take place?

Step 4: Is there anything from this passage that is confusing? Write down any questions from this passage you have for your mentor, friend, or pastor?

Step 5: Application: What will you do differently in your life and walk with Christ because of this passage?

Step 6: Pray to close your time with God. Ask for Him to help you continue to understand scripture and to apply what you just read in His Word.

DAY 4 BIBLE READING PLAN

Read - Ephesians 5:8-14

Step 1: As you open your bible to Mark pray to open your time with God. Ask Him to show you truth as you read Scripture today.

Step 2: Read Ephesians 5:8-14 and underline any verses that stick out to you. Write down those verses here:

Step 3: Make observations:

Who is in this passage?

What is going on?

Where does it take place?

Step 4: Is there anything from this passage that is confusing? Write down any questions from this passage you have for your mentor, friend, or pastor?

Step 5: Application: What will you do differently in your life and walk with Christ because of this passage?

Step 6: Pray to close your time with God. Ask for Him to help you continue to understand scripture and to apply what you just read in His Word.

DAY 5 BIBLE READING PLAN

Read - Ephesians 5:15-20

Step 1: As you open your bible to Mark pray to open your time with God. Ask Him to show you truth as you read Scripture today.

Step 2: Read Ephesians 5:15-20 and underline any verses that stick out to you. Write down those verses here:

Step 3: Make observations:

Who is in this passage?

What is going on?

Where does it take place?

Step 4: Is there anything from this passage that is confusing? Write down any questions from this passage you have for your mentor, friend, or pastor?

Step 5: Application: What will you do differently in your life and walk with Christ because of this passage?

Step 6: Pray to close your time with God. Ask for Him to help you continue to understand scripture and to apply what you just read in His Word.

DAY 6 BIBLE READING PLAN

Read - Ephesians 5:21-27

Step 1: As you open your bible to Mark pray to open your time with God. Ask Him to show you truth as you read Scripture today.

Step 2: Read Ephesians 5:21-27 and underline any verses that stick out to you. Write down those verses here:

Step 3: Make observations:

Who is in this passage?

What is going on?

Where does it take place?

Step 4: Is there anything from this passage that is confusing? Write down any questions from this passage you have for your mentor, friend, or pastor?

Step 5: Application: What will you do differently in your life and walk with Christ because of this passage?

Step 6: Pray to close your time with God. Ask for Him to help you continue to understand scripture and to apply what you just read in His Word.

DAY 7 BIBLE READING PLAN

Read - Ephesians 5:28-33

Step 1: As you open your bible to Mark pray to open your time with God. Ask Him to show you truth as you read Scripture today.

Step 2: Read Ephesians 5:28-33 and underline any verses that stick out to you. Write down those verses here:

Step 3: Make observations:

Who is in this passage?

What is going on?

Where does it take place?

Step 4: Is there anything from this passage that is confusing? Write down any questions from this passage you have for your mentor, friend, or pastor?

Step 5: Application: What will you do differently in your life and walk with Christ because of this passage?

Step 6: Pray to close your time with God. Ask for Him to help you continue to understand scripture and to apply what you just read in His Word.

WEEK 10 TRAINING: HOLY SPIRIT

How would you describe the Holy Spirit?

Read Ephesians 1:13

We receive the Holy Spirit at the moment of our _____.

Read John 14:26

The Holy Spirit is our _____, _____, and _____.

Read John 16:8

One of the Holy Spirit's roles is to _____ _____ _____ of sin.

It is not our _____ to _____ the world of _____.

Read John 15:26

The Holy Spirit points to the _____ about _____.

How do you know if you are filled with the Holy Spirit?

Read Ephesians 5:18

Being filled means that we are _____ by the _____ _____.

It means that we are saying _____ to the flesh and _____ to God.

Read Galatians 5:22-23

We know that we are filled because of our _____ with _____.

Read 1 Corinthians 12:7-11

We know that we are filled because of our _____ for _____

Read Acts 1:8

We know that we are filled because of our _____ for _____.[1]

Questions:

Has your view of the Holy Spirit changed?

What questions do you still have about the Holy Spirit?

Here are a few resources to understand who the Holy Spirit is:

Book - *Forgotten God*
   https://bit.ly/frgttngod

Book - *How to be Filled With the Holy Spirit*
   https://bit.ly/filledwhs

DAY 1 BIBLE READING PLAN

Read - Ephesians 6:1-9

Step 1: As you open your bible to Mark pray to open your time with God. Ask Him to show you truth as you read Scripture today.

Step 2: Read Ephesians 6:1-9 and underline any verses that stick out to you. Write down those verses here:

Step 3: Make observations:

Who is in this passage?

What is going on?

Where does it take place?

Step 4: Is there anything from this passage that is confusing? Write down any questions from this passage you have for your mentor, friend, or pastor?

Step 5: Application: What will you do differently in your life and walk with Christ because of this passage?

Step 6: Pray to close your time with God. Ask for Him to help you continue to understand scripture and to apply what you just read in His Word.

DAY 2 BIBLE READING PLAN

Read - Ephesians 6:10-23

Step 1: As you open your bible to Mark pray to open your time with God. Ask Him to show you truth as you read Scripture today.

Step 2: Read Ephesians 6:10-23 and underline any verses that stick out to you. Write down those verses here:

Step 3: Make observations:

Who is in this passage?

What is going on?

Where does it take place?

Step 4: Is there anything from this passage that is confusing? Write down any questions from this passage you have for your mentor, friend, or pastor?

Step 5: Application: What will you do differently in your life and walk with Christ because of this passage?

Step 6: Pray to close your time with God. Ask for Him to help you continue to understand scripture and to apply what you just read in His Word.

DAY 3 BIBLE READING PLAN

Read - Philippians 1:1-11

Step 1: As you open your bible to Mark pray to open your time with God. Ask Him to show you truth as you read Scripture today.

Step 2: Watch this introduction video to Philippians: https://bit.ly/philippiansintro

Step 3 Read Philippians 1:1-11 and underline any verses that stick out to you. Write down those verses here:

Step 4: Make observations:

Who is in this passage?

What is going on?

Where does it take place?

Step 5: Is there anything from this passage that is confusing? Write down any questions from this passage you have for your mentor, friend, or pastor?

Step 6: Application: What will you do differently in your life and walk with Christ because of this passage?

Step 7: Pray to close your time with God. Ask for Him to help you continue to understand scripture and to apply what you just read in His Word.

DAY 4 BIBLE READING PLAN

Read - Philippians 1:12-19

Step 1: As you open your bible to Mark pray to open your time with God. Ask Him to show you truth as you read Scripture today.

Step 2: Read Philippians 1:12-19 and underline any verses that stick out to you. Write down those verses here:

Step 3: Make observations:

Who is in this passage?

What is going on?

Where does it take place?

Step 4: Is there anything from this passage that is confusing? Write down any questions from this passage you have for your mentor, friend, or pastor?

Step 5: Application: What will you do differently in your life and walk with Christ because of this passage?

Step 6: Pray to close your time with God. Ask for Him to help you continue to understand scripture and to apply what you just read in His Word.

DAY 5 BIBLE READING PLAN

Read - Philippians 1:20-26

Step 1: As you open your bible to Mark pray to open your time with God. Ask Him to show you truth as you read Scripture today.

Step 2: Read Philippians 1:20-26 and underline any verses that stick out to you. Write down those verses here:

Step 3: Make observations:

Who is in this passage?

What is going on?

Where does it take place?

Step 4: Is there anything from this passage that is confusing? Write down any questions from this passage you have for your mentor, friend, or pastor?

Step 5: Application: What will you do differently in your life and walk with Christ because of this passage?

Step 6: Pray to close your time with God. Ask for Him to help you continue to understand scripture and to apply what you just read in His Word.

DAY 6 BIBLE READING PLAN

Read - Philippians 1:27-30

Step 1: As you open your bible to Mark pray to open your time with God. Ask Him to show you truth as you read Scripture today.

Step 2: Read Philippians 1:27-30 and underline any verses that stick out to you. Write down those verses here:

Step 3: Make observations:

Who is in this passage?

What is going on?

Where does it take place?

Step 4: Is there anything from this passage that is confusing? Write down any questions from this passage you have for your mentor, friend, or pastor?

Step 5: Application: What will you do differently in your life and walk with Christ because of this passage?

Step 6: Pray to close your time with God. Ask for Him to help you continue to understand scripture and to apply what you just read in His Word.

DAY 7 BIBLE READING PLAN

Read - Philippians 2:1-4

Step 1: As you open your bible to Mark pray to open your time with God. Ask Him to show you truth as you read Scripture today.

Step 2: Read Philippians 2:1-4 and underline any verses that stick out to you. Write down those verses here:

Step 3: Make observations:

Who is in this passage?

What is going on?

Where does it take place?

Step 4: Is there anything from this passage that is confusing? Write down any questions from this passage you have for your mentor, friend, or pastor?

Step 5: Application: What will you do differently in your life and walk with Christ because of this passage?

Step 6: Pray to close your time with God. Ask for Him to help you continue to understand scripture and to apply what you just read in His Word.

WEEK 11 TRAINING: COMMUNITY

Read Romans 12:5 and Ephesians 1:22-23

The Bible describes the relationship between _____ and the _____ as a _____.

Read Acts 2:42-47

The Church is a group of _____ meeting together around the truth of the _____.

We can't follow _____ outside of a _____ _____ _____.

What are the functions of a church?

Hebrews 10:24

Matthew 28:20

Psalms 149:1

Ephesians 4:12

Activities within the Church[1]

Baptism

Read 1 Peter 3:21

Baptism _____ our lives that have been _____ cleansed by the death of Jesus.

Communion

Read Matthew 26:17-19, 26-30

Jesus told us that _____ is representative of His _____ _____

We take communion in _____ of His _____ and _____.

Read 1 Corinthians 11:23-29

We must _____ our _____ _____ _____ before we take _____.

Tithes and Offerings

Read Genesis 14:19-20

The word _____ literally means _____.

This is the first _____ in scripture.

From this point on we see throughout the _____ _____ that tithing was a _____.

Read Matthew 23:23

You should have practiced _____, _____, and _____ without stopping the _____.

Questions:

Have you found Christian community?

What has been difficult about developing community?

Do you struggle with tithing? If so why do you believe that is?

Here is a resource to go deeper:

Book - *Life Together*
    https://bit.ly/lftogether

DAY 1 BIBLE READING PLAN

Read - Philippians 2:25-30

Step 1: As you open your bible to Mark pray to open your time with God. Ask Him to show you truth as you read Scripture today.

Step 2: Read Philippians 2:25-30 and underline any verses that stick out to you. Write down those verses here:

Step 3: Make observations:

Who is in this passage?

What is going on?

Where does it take place?

Step 4: Is there anything from this passage that is confusing? Write down any questions from this passage you have for your mentor, friend, or pastor?

Step 5: Application: What will you do differently in your life and walk with Christ because of this passage?

Step 6: Pray to close your time with God. Ask for Him to help you continue to understand scripture and to apply what you just read in His Word.

DAY 2 BIBLE READING PLAN

Read - Philippians 2:12-18

Step 1: As you open your bible to Mark pray to open your time with God. Ask Him to show you truth as you read Scripture today.

Step 2: Read Philippians 2:12-18 and underline any verses that stick out to you. Write down those verses here:

Step 3: Make observations:

Who is in this passage?

What is going on?

Where does it take place?

Step 4: Is there anything from this passage that is confusing? Write down any questions from this passage you have for your mentor, friend, or pastor?

Step 5: Application: What will you do differently in your life and walk with Christ because of this passage?

Step 6: Pray to close your time with God. Ask for Him to help you continue to understand scripture and to apply what you just read in His Word.

DAY 3 BIBLE READING PLAN

Read - Philippians 2:19-24

Step 1: As you open your bible to Mark pray to open your time with God. Ask Him to show you truth as you read Scripture today.

Step 2: Read Philippians 2:19-24 and underline any verses that stick out to you. Write down those verses here:

Step 3: Make observations:

Who is in this passage?

What is going on?

Where does it take place?

Step 4: Is there anything from this passage that is confusing? Write down any questions from this passage you have for your mentor, friend, or pastor?

Step 5: Application: What will you do differently in your life and walk with Christ because of this passage?

Step 6: Pray to close your time with God. Ask for Him to help you continue to understand scripture and to apply what you just read in His Word.

DAY 4 BIBLE READING PLAN

Read - Philippians 2:5-11

Step 1: As you open your bible to Mark pray to open your time with God. Ask Him to show you truth as you read Scripture today.

Step 2: Read Philippians 2:5-11 and underline any verses that stick out to you. Write down those verses here:

Step 3: Make observations:

Who is in this passage?

What is going on?

Where does it take place?

Step 4: Is there anything from this passage that is confusing? Write down any questions from this passage you have for your mentor, friend, or pastor?

Step 5: Application: What will you do differently in your life and walk with Christ because of this passage?

Step 6: Pray to close your time with God. Ask for Him to help you continue to understand scripture and to apply what you just read in His Word.

DAY 5 BIBLE READING PLAN

Read - Philippians 3:1-4

Step 1: As you open your bible to Mark pray to open your time with God. Ask Him to show you truth as you read Scripture today.

Step 2: Read Philippians 3:1-4 and underline any verses that stick out to you. Write down those verses here:

Step 3: Make observations:

Who is in this passage?

What is going on?

Where does it take place?

Step 4: Is there anything from this passage that is confusing? Write down any questions from this passage you have for your mentor, friend, or pastor?

Step 5: Application: What will you do differently in your life and walk with Christ because of this passage?

Step 6: Pray to close your time with God. Ask for Him to help you continue to understand scripture and to apply what you just read in His Word.

DAY 6 BIBLE READING PLAN

Read - Philippians 3:5-11

Step 1: As you open your bible to Mark pray to open your time with God. Ask Him to show you truth as you read Scripture today.

Step 2: Read Philippians 3:5-11 and underline any verses that stick out to you. Write down those verses here:

Step 3: Make observations:

Who is in this passage?

What is going on?

Where does it take place?

Step 4: Is there anything from this passage that is confusing? Write down any questions from this passage you have for your mentor, friend, or pastor?

Step 5: Application: What will you do differently in your life and walk with Christ because of this passage?

Step 6: Pray to close your time with God. Ask for Him to help you continue to understand scripture and to apply what you just read in His Word.

DAY 7 BIBLE READING PLAN

Read – Philippians 3:12-14

Step 1: As you open your bible to Mark pray to open your time with God. Ask Him to show you truth as you read Scripture today.

Step 2: Read Philippians 3:12-14 and underline any verses that stick out to you. Write down those verses here:

Step 3: Make observations:

Who is in this passage?

What is going on?

Where does it take place?

Step 4: Is there anything from this passage that is confusing? Write down any questions from this passage you have for your mentor, friend, or pastor?

Step 5: Application: What will you do differently in your life and walk with Christ because of this passage?

Step 6: Pray to close your time with God. Ask for Him to help you continue to understand scripture and to apply what you just read in His Word.

WEEK 12 TRAINING: SPIRITUAL DISCIPLINES

Read 1 Timothy 4:7

Giving

Read Luke 6:37-38

Read 2 Corinthians 9:7

How are we supposed to give?

There are various other offerings and giving talked about in scripture

In your own time read Proverbs 3:9-10, Matthew 6:1-4, Mark 12:41-44

Fasting

Read Matthew 4:1-2

Read Acts 13:2

Read Daniel 10:3

_____ is a spiritual discipline where you _____ from something like _____ for a period of _____.

Sabbath

Read Genesis 2:1-3

God instituted a _____ of _____ at the beginning of Creation.

Read Mark 2:23-28

God created the sabbath for _____ not for Himself

Scripture Memory

Read Matthew 4:4

Read Psalm 119:11

Read Colossians 3:16

God's _____ is our spiritual food, and _____
_____ helps capture it in our _____.

Questions:

Which of these spiritual disciplines do you struggle with the most and why?

How can you make an effort to be better in this area of struggle?

Here is a resource to go deeper:

Book - *Spiritual Disciplines*
https://bit.ly/sprtdisciplines

DAY 1 BIBLE READING PLAN

Read - Philippians 3:15-21

Step 1: As you open your bible to Mark pray to open your time with God. Ask Him to show you truth as you read Scripture today.

Step 2: Read Philippians 3:15-21 and underline any verses that stick out to you. Write down those verses here:

Step 3: Make observations:

Who is in this passage?

What is going on?

Where does it take place?

Step 4: Is there anything from this passage that is confusing? Write down any questions from this passage you have for your mentor, friend, or pastor?

Step 5: Application: What will you do differently in your life and walk with Christ because of this passage?

Step 6: Pray to close your time with God. Ask for Him to help you continue to understand scripture and to apply what you just read in His Word.

DAY 2 BIBLE READING PLAN

Read - Philippians 4:1-3

Step 1: As you open your bible to Mark pray to open your time with God. Ask Him to show you truth as you read Scripture today.

Step 2: Read Philippians 4:1-3 and underline any verses that stick out to you. Write down those verses here:

Step 3: Make observations:

Who is in this passage?

What is going on?

Where does it take place?

Step 4: Is there anything from this passage that is confusing? Write down any questions from this passage you have for your mentor, friend, or pastor?

Step 5: Application: What will you do differently in your life and walk with Christ because of this passage?

Step 6: Pray to close your time with God. Ask for Him to help you continue to understand scripture and to apply what you just read in His Word.

DAY 3 BIBLE READING PLAN

Read - Philippians 4:4-7

Step 1: As you open your bible to Mark pray to open your time with God. Ask Him to show you truth as you read Scripture today.

Step 2: Read Philippians 4:4-7 and underline any verses that stick out to you. Write down those verses here:

Step 3: Make observations:

Who is in this passage?

What is going on?

Where does it take place?

Step 4: Is there anything from this passage that is confusing? Write down any questions from this passage you have for your mentor, friend, or pastor?

Step 5: Application: What will you do differently in your life and walk with Christ because of this passage?

Step 6: Pray to close your time with God. Ask for Him to help you continue to understand scripture and to apply what you just read in His Word.

DAY 4 BIBLE READING PLAN

Read - Philippians 4:8-9

Step 1: As you open your bible to Mark pray to open your time with God. Ask Him to show you truth as you read Scripture today.

Step 2: Read Philippians 4:8-9 and underline any verses that stick out to you. Write down those verses here:

Step 3: Make observations:

Who is in this passage?

What is going on?

Where does it take place?

Step 4: Is there anything from this passage that is confusing? Write down any questions from this passage you have for your mentor, friend, or pastor?

Step 5: Application: What will you do differently in your life and walk with Christ because of this passage?

Step 6: Pray to close your time with God. Ask for Him to help you continue to understand scripture and to apply what you just read in His Word.

DAY 5 BIBLE READING PLAN

Read - Philippians 4:10-13

Step 1: As you open your bible to Mark pray to open your time with God. Ask Him to show you truth as you read Scripture today.

Step 2: Read Philippians 4:10-13 and underline any verses that stick out to you. Write down those verses here:

Step 3: Make observations:

Who is in this passage?

What is going on?

Where does it take place?

Step 4: Is there anything from this passage that is confusing? Write down any questions from this passage you have for your mentor, friend, or pastor?

Step 5: Application: What will you do differently in your life and walk with Christ because of this passage?

Step 6: Pray to close your time with God. Ask for Him to help you continue to understand scripture and to apply what you just read in His Word.

DAY 6 BIBLE READING PLAN

Read - Philippians 4:14-16

Step 1: As you open your bible to Mark pray to open your time with God. Ask Him to show you truth as you read Scripture today.

Step 2: Read Philippians 4:14-16 and underline any verses that stick out to you. Write down those verses here:

Step 3: Make observations:

Who is in this passage?

What is going on?

Where does it take place?

Step 4: Is there anything from this passage that is confusing? Write down any questions from this passage you have for your mentor, friend, or pastor?

Step 5: Application: What will you do differently in your life and walk with Christ because of this passage?

Step 6: Pray to close your time with God. Ask for Him to help you continue to understand scripture and to apply what you just read in His Word.

DAY 7 BIBLE READING PLAN

Read - Philippians 4:17-24

Step 1: As you open your bible to Mark pray to open your time with God. Ask Him to show you truth as you read Scripture today.

Step 2: Read Philippians 4:17-24 and underline any verses that stick out to you. Write down those verses here:

Step 3: Make observations:

Who is in this passage?

What is going on?

Where does it take place?

Step 4: Is there anything from this passage that is confusing? Write down any questions from this passage you have for your mentor, friend, or pastor?

Step 5: Application: What will you do differently in your life and walk with Christ because of this passage?

Step 6: Pray to close your time with God. Ask for Him to help you continue to understand scripture and to apply what you just read in His Word.

WEEK 13 TRAINING: GRACE

Read Ephesians 2:8-10 & 1 Corinthians 15:10

It is by _____ you have been saved.

Not only does _____ save us but grace _____ us to live our Christian life.

As we go about discipleship, we must remember that we are to celebrate that our names are _____ in heaven.

Read 1 Corinthians 3:1-9

So, who did what exactly?

We _____ _____ supposed to _____ about who is doing a certain part of discipleship.

Questions:

How have you seen God move in your life over the last few months?

Do you struggle with giving yourself grace? If yes, why do you believe that is?

WHAT'S NEXT

Before we go any further, I just want to take a moment and say that I am so proud of you for finishing this training. Over the past three months you have been going through a lot of teachings about Jesus and our faith in Him! This is no small feat! As we finish this curriculum, remember that we are setting out to launch a movement of disciple-makers.

The 13 teachings you received in this training are created for you to teach others so that they can teach others too! Don't give up helping others start making disciples by using this material over and over again!

As you finish the final training, make sure you go through these next steps with your group. Make a plan to take the next steps in your life as you continue to grow in your relationship with God. Use the resources mentioned below or find others to continue growing as a disciple of Christ.

1) Continue to read God's Word! My hope and prayer for you is that at some point in the near future you will end up reading through the entire bible. You already have finished 3 books in 3 months! There are many great reading plans but now that you have learned how to dive

into it a few verses at a time you can do it yourself. Grab a small journal off a shelf at a store and continue to read God's Word!

2) Continue Godly Community - When you finish this training it does not mean that you are done with your discipleship relationship. Discipleship isn't a 3 month program. This training is to just help get started! Not only do you need a discipleship relationship, but you also need the entire body of Christ. If you are not already connected to a church family, make sure you plug in to one as soon as you can!

3) Continue Character Development - We are supposed to become more and more like Jesus. Therefore, we must know who we are in order for us to walk out who God has created us to be. Here are a few more resources to help you discover who God has created you to be:

Emotionally Healthy Spirituality – There are a ton of resources for this material. There are multiple books, videos, and devotionals to help you get started on an emotionally healthy journey. If you were to pick one thing out of all of these resources to start with, I would suggest this book and their resources.

No Longer Labeled – Find out how to shed your old identities and find out who God called you to be.

Sit Walk Stand - This book is another great resource to discover who God called you to be!

A Work of Heart - This book talks about the past of major Bible characters and how each of their pasts shaped them into the person God called them to be!

4) More Discipleship Resources - Look at these amazing trainings and resources for continuing to make disciples of Jesus.

Training For Trainers - This resource was influential in the shaping of this book and material. The book talks about how to shape and form disciple making movements.

Real Life Discipleship - Another great resource that help shape some of the content in this training. It is very detailed and great for going deep with discipleship

The Lost Art of Disciplemaking – If you want to be convicted about discipleship this is a great book to study in greater detail!

The Master Plan of Evangelism - This is one of the most widely used and respected book when it comes to discipleship. If you haven't read and used this in your training to make disciples, don't miss out on this important book.

Multiply- This book covers a ton about discipleship. It talks about God's Word, how to read the Old Testament and New Testament, and much, much more!

Discipled by Jesus - This is the ultimate aim for us as we make disciples. We hope and pray that the people we help disciple would be lifelong apprentices of Jesus. This is a great resource to read as a group.

5) Other great books:
Worship as Work
Every Good Endeavor
The Fuel & the Flame
Emotionally Healthy Discipleship
Deep Discipleship

CHEAT SHEET: WEEK 1: SALVATION

God's Design - Read Genesis 1

As God designed all of the world, He looked upon it and saw it was good.

He designed us for relationship with him and with a mission in this world.

Sin & Brokenness - Read Genesis 3

Because of Adam and Eve's sin we all face the brokenness and consequences

This is the reason for not only our own personal sin. But also, all of the brokenness that we see in the world today.

The result of sin is <u>separation from God</u>.

Gospel - Read Luke 19:1-10

Jesus came to <u>seek</u> and <u>save</u> the <u>lost</u>

Because of Jesus' <u>sacrifice</u> on the <u>cross</u> we can now have an <u>intimate relationship</u> with God.

Read Romans 10:9-10

If we confess Jesus as our <u>Lord</u> and believe He was raised from the <u>dead</u> we will be saved.

Recover & Pursue - Read 2 Corinthians 5:16-21

If anyone is in Christ, they are a <u>new creation.</u> The <u>old</u> has gone, the <u>new</u> has come.

Because of our salvation our lives have been <u>changed</u>. This means we are able to no longer <u>live</u> the way we did before our lives with Christ!

Grace - Read Ephesians 2:8-10

It is by <u>grace</u> that we have been saved.

We are created for <u>good works</u> which God prepared in advance for us to do.

Extra Studying: This week read the accounts of Jesus' death and resurrection.
    Matthew 27-28
    Mark 15-16
    Luke 23-24
    John 18-20

CHEAT SHEET WEEK 2: BAPTISM

Read Matthew 3:13-17

Jesus <u>modeled</u> the <u>importance</u> of baptism for us.

Baptism is the <u>public</u> declaration of our inward <u>commitment</u>.

We are told in Matthew 28 that we supposed to <u>baptize</u> all who are disciples of Jesus.

<u>Everyone</u> who believes in Christ should be <u>baptized</u>.

Symbolic of our life with Christ

Us going into and under the water is symbolic of our <u>death</u>

Us being raised out of the water is symbolic for our resurrection.

Read Luke 23:32-43

After reading this passage do you believe you have to be baptized in order to be saved? Why or why not?

CHEAT SHEET WEEK 3: BIBLE STUDY

Read 2 Timothy 3:16-17

Scripture is sufficient for all we need to walk out our faith in Jesus Christ.

Scripture is also our authority.

Read Psalms 119:147-148

Scripture is essential for our relationship with God.

Read Psalms 119:105

God's Word will guide us in the way He designed us to live.

CHEAT SHEET WEEK 4: PRAYER

Read Luke 18:1

Jesus tells us we should always pray.

Read Matthew 6:5-15

Jesus modeled for us a deep life of prayer.

We shouldn't pray like others around us who are looking for recognition.

Prayer is designed to help us develop a deep relationship with God.

How then does Jesus tell us to pray?

Types of Prayers

Requests Read Philippians 4:6-7

Thanksgiving Read 1 Timothy 2:1 & Philippians 4:6-7

Praise Read Psalm 135:3

Confession Read James 5:16

CHEAT SHEET WEEK 5: VISION

Read Matthew 4:18-22

One of the first things that Jesus did after his baptism (Matthew 3) was go find disciples.

Jesus told them to follow me and I will make you fishers of men.

Jesus describing to them the two biggest things when it comes to discipleship:
1) Intimacy with God.
2) Making disciples.

Read Matthew 28:18-20

Because all authority has been given to Jesus we are supposed to make disciples.

What does making disciples look like according to this passage?

1) Make disciples.
2) Baptize them.
3) Teach them to obey His commands.

Jesus leaves us with a promise at the end of this passage what is it?

He will be with us

Read Acts 1:1-11

Where was God sending the disciples?

Jerusalem - Home Town
Judea - State or Province
Samaria - Neighboring States/Provinces
The Ends of the Earth - The entire world

Read 2 Timothy 2:1-2

Vision for discipleship is to the 4th generation

- Paul Discipled Timothy
- Timothy disciples reliable people
- Reliable people disciple others

What if 10 people started discipled 2 people a year?

How many people would we reach in:
    5 years 320
    10 years 10,240 - Half of Hays Kansas
    25 years 335 Million - population of USA
    30 years over 7 billion - population of world

CHEAT SHEET WEEK 6: EVANGELISM

Read Matthew 13:1-23

What are the 4 types of Seeds?

1) Seed on the Path

2) Seed on Rocky Soil

3) Seed Among Thorns

4) Good Soil

<u>Evangelism</u> looks a lot like us sowing seeds in the <u>world</u> around us.

Don't be surprised as you share the Gospel if this parable comes to life.

Our job is not to worry about people's response but to sow seeds.

Read: John 4:1-42

No one can argue with your testimony.

What if sharing the Gospel is as easy as sharing your story?

Read Luke 10:1-20

Sharing the Gospel simply starts with a relationship with Jesus

CHEAT SHEET WEEK 7: INTIMATE RELATIONSHIP

Read John 5:16-23

Jesus <u>modeled</u> for us what an <u>intimate relationship</u> with God can look like.

Jesus again connects our <u>relationship</u> with God with our <u>works</u>

This doesn't mean that our <u>works</u> will <u>save us</u>. But it does mean that because of our <u>love</u> for God we will walk in <u>obedience</u>.

Read John 15:1-17

What does Jesus use to illustrate our relationship with Him?

Vine & branches

What do you think it means to abide (remain)?

Abiding is an ever growing, continual relationship with God.

Once again Jesus connects our obedience to Him to our relationship with Him.

CHEAT SHEET WEEK 8: GOD THE FATHER

Read 1 John 3:1

We have a Heavenly Father who <u>lavishes</u> His <u>love</u> on us.

Read Matthew 7:7-12

What stands out to you about God the Father in this passage? Does this change your perspective of Him?

Read Luke 15:11-24

No matter <u>how far</u> you have fallen away from God the Father, He will always <u>celebrate your return</u>

Read Proverbs 3:11-12

In His love God will discipline His Children.

CHEAT SHEET WEEK 9: JESUS

Read Matthew 16:13-21

There is a difference between the way the world views Jesus and who He really is.

Read John 1:35-39

Jesus is our teacher

Read Philippians 2:8-11, Revelation 19:16

Jesus is our Lord and King

Read John 3:16, 1 John 4:14

Jesus is our Savior

Read John 10:1-18

Jesus is our Shepherd

Read John 1:1, 1:14, Romans 9:5

Jesus is God

CHEAT SHEET WEEK 10: HOLY SPIRIT

Read Ephesians 1:13

We receive the Holy Spirit at the moment of our Salvation.

Read John 14:26 ESV

The Holy Spirit is our helper, advocate, and comforter.

Read John 16:8

One of the Holy Spirit's roles is to convict the world of sin.

It is not our job to convict the world of sin.

Read John 15:26

The Holy Spirit points to the truth about Jesus.

How do you know if you are filled with the Holy Spirit?

Read Ephesians 5:18

Being filled means that we are controlled by the Holy Spirit.

It means that we are saying no to the flesh and yes to God.

Read Galatians 5:22-23

We know that we are filled because of our walk with God.

Read 1 Corinthians 12:7-14

We know that we are filled because of our work for God.

Read Acts 1:8

We know that we are filled because of our witness for God.

CHEAT SHEET WEEK 11: COMMUNITY

Read Romans 12:5 and Ephesians 1:22-23

The Bible describes the relationship between <u>Jesus</u> and the <u>Church</u> as a <u>body</u>

Read Acts 2:42-47

The church is a group of <u>people</u> meeting together around the truth of the <u>gospel</u>

We can't follow <u>Jesus</u> outside of a <u>group of people</u>

What are the functions of a church?

Hebrews 10:24
 (Fellowship)

Matthew 28:20
 (Teaching)

Read Psalms 149:1
 (Worship)

Ephesians 4:12
 (Ministry)

1) Baptism

Read 1 Peter 3:21

Baptism symbolizes our lives that have been spiritually cleansed by the death of Jesus.

2) Communion

Read Matthew 26:17-19, 26-30

Jesus told us that communion is representative of His new covenant.

We take communion in remembrance of His death and resurrection

Read 1 Corinthians 11:23-29

We must examine our faith and actions before we take communion

3) Tithing and Offerings

Read Genesis 14:19-20

The word tithe literally means tenth

This is the first tithe in scripture

From this point on we see throughout the Old Testament that tithing was a command.

Read Matthew 23:23

You should have practiced justice, mercy, and faithfulness without stopping the tithe

CHEAT SHEET WEEK 12: SPIRITUAL DISCIPLINES

Read 1 Timothy 4:7

1) Giving

Read Luke 6:37-38

Read 2 Corinthians 9:7

How are we supposed to give?

Generously & Cheerfully

There are various other offerings and giving talked about in scripture:

In your own time read Proverbs 3:9-10, Matthew 6:1-4, Mark 12:41-44

2) Fasting

Read Matthew 4:1-2

Read Acts 13:2

Read Daniel 10:3

Fasting is a spiritual discipline where you abstain from something like food for a period of time

3) Sabbath

Read Genesis 2:1-3

God instituted a day of rest at the beginning of Creation.

Read Mark 2:23-28

God created the sabbath for man not for Himself

4) Scripture Memory

Read Matthew 4:4

Read Psalm 119:11

Read Colossians 3:16

God's <u>Word</u> is our spiritual food, and <u>memorizing scripture</u> helps capture it in our <u>hearts</u>.

CHEAT SHEET WEEK 13: GRACE

Read Ephesians 2:8-10 & 1 Corinthians 15:10

It is by grace you have been saved.

Not only does grace save us but grace empowers us to live our Christian life.

As we go about discipleship, we must remember that we are to celebrate that our names are written in heaven.

Read 1 Corinthians 3:1-9

So, who did what exactly?

Paul planted, Apollos watered, and God made it grow!

We are not supposed to worry about who is doing a certain part of discipleship.

NOTES

WEEK 4 TRAINING: PRAYER

1. Kai, Ying, and Grace Kai. "Free T4T Lesson Downloads in 12 Different Languages." T4T Global. Accessed June 14, 2021. https://www.t4tglobal.org/t4t-lessons.

WEEK 10 TRAINING: HOLY SPIRIT

1. Jones, Bill, and Terry Powell. *Walking In the Spirit*. Christians Publications, 2001.

WEEK 11 TRAINING: COMMUNITY

1. Kai, Ying, and Grace Kai. "Free T4T Lesson Downloads in 12 Different Languages." T4T Global. Accessed June 14, 2021. https://www.t4tglobal.org/t4t-lessons.

Made in the USA
Thornton, CO
05/27/24 18:55:54

0d9f50e0-adbd-4785-b278-07613386a2bbR01